NATIONAL
GEOGRAPHIC
Oak

D1220181

Sharks

Pamela Rushby

Contents

Great white sharks can ▶
be 21 feet long.

The World of Sharks

Of all the fish in the sea, sharks are probably the scariest and the most misunderstood. When most people think of sharks, they imagine huge fish with rows of razor-sharp teeth. Some sharks, such as the great white shark, are like that. But there are many different kinds of sharks. Most of them are no danger to humans at all.

Types of Sharks

Sharks come in all shapes and sizes. Some are small enough to hold in your hand. Others are bigger than a large truck. The size and shape of a shark's body depends on which part of the ocean it lives in and what it eats.

▲ The whale shark is the largest shark in the sea. It measures almost 60 feet long.

The goblin shark lives ▶
very deep in the ocean.
It is hardly ever seen.

▲ The thresher shark beats the water with its long tail fin.
This causes other fish to move so it can catch them.

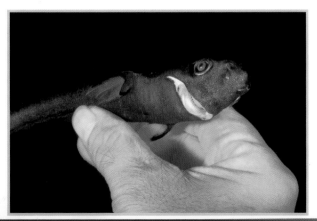

◀ The pygmy shark is one
of the smallest in the
ocean. It is only about
eight inches long.

Perfect Predators

All sharks have one thing in common. Sharks are predators. This means they hunt and eat other animals. Sharks have special features that help them hunt and catch their prey, or food. Most sharks eat seals and other fish. Some sharks eat tiny sea creatures that float in the water.

Sharks can hunt in groups and work together to catch their prey.

Creature Feature

Wobbegong Shark

The wobbegong shark's flat shape and rock-like markings help this shark to hide on the bottom of the ocean. The wobbegong shark hides until its prey comes near. Then it dashes out to catch its meal.

Shark Teeth

The shape of a shark's teeth depends on the kind of food it eats. The great white shark has sharp teeth with jagged edges. Whale sharks have very small teeth because they don't bite the tiny sea creatures they eat. They swallow them whole.

Sharks grow new teeth all the time. A shark's jaws are lined with five or more rows of teeth. When a shark's tooth becomes worn, it falls out. A new tooth moves forward to replace the lost one.

The great white shark has sharp teeth and a wide jaw.

Creature Feature

Basking Shark

The basking shark is the second largest shark in the sea. It can grow up to 40 feet long. A shark this big sounds scary, but the good news is that the basking shark is harmless. It has very small teeth that are not sharp.

Shark Senses

Sharks have the same senses that you do. They hear, smell, feel, see, and taste. They use all these senses to survive in the sea.

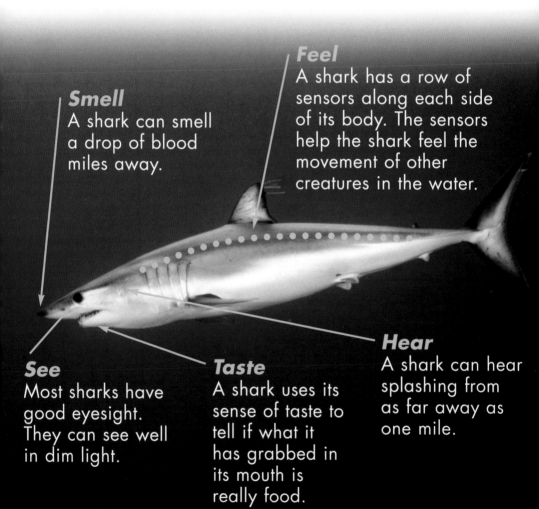

Feel
A shark has a row of sensors along each side of its body. The sensors help the shark feel the movement of other creatures in the water.

Smell
A shark can smell a drop of blood miles away.

See
Most sharks have good eyesight. They can see well in dim light.

Taste
A shark uses its sense of taste to tell if what it has grabbed in its mouth is really food.

Hear
A shark can hear splashing from as far away as one mile.

Creature Feature

Hammerhead Shark

It's easy to see how the hammerhead shark got its name. The unusual shape of its head helps the hammerhead shark hunt for food. Having an eye and nostril on each side of its wide, thick head helps the hammerhead shark steer through the water.

Sharks and People

When you go to the beach, could you be attacked by a shark? It's very unlikely. Only a few types of sharks attack humans, and it's probably a mistake when they do. The shark may mistake a person for a seal or some other kind of food.

People are far more dangerous to sharks than sharks are to people. Hunters kill millions of sharks each year. Other sharks die from polluted waters.

Special divers trained to handle sharks help us learn more about shark behavior.

Creature Feature

Great White Shark

The most dangerous shark to humans is the great white. Worldwide, there have been 205 recorded attacks on humans by great whites since 1876. However, people are far more likely to die from a bee sting or a lightning strike than a shark attack.

People now know that even though some sharks are scary, they play an important role in the ocean. As predators, they keep the sea clean by killing off weak and sick animals. To protect sharks, laws have been passed making it illegal to hunt sharks in certain parts of the ocean.

When you see a shark in an aquarium, think about how the shark's shape, teeth, and senses help it live in the ocean. You'll know that you are looking at one of the world's most amazing creatures.

Aquariums are good places to see sharks up close.

Creature Feature

Tiger Shark

Most sharks will spit out something that doesn't taste good, but a tiger shark isn't very choosy about what it eats. All kinds of strange things have been found in the stomachs of tiger sharks, including plastic bags, pieces of wood, and tin cans.

Index